PIRATES
MAGNIFIED

WIDE EYED EDITIONS

As you journey through the pages of this book, you'll discover the lives of 10 real pirates, learn about life on the high seas—both above and below deck—and explore some of the key moments in pirating history in the minutest of detail.

Meet Blackbeard with his burning fuses on the high seas; James Ford, who was court judge by day and river pirate by night; and Anne Bonny and Mary Read, who proved that female pirates could be just as feisty as any man.

HOW TO USE THIS BOOK

Turn the page and soak up the action before your eyes . . . Each time you revisit a scene, you'll see something new! Read the text and find out what's happening. Which pirate is stealing from the sailors, looting from the locals, or making merry with the merchants' booty?

Next, grab your magnifying glass and see if you can spot the 10 items described on each page. Take a close look at each action-packed scene and cutaway illustration. You'll find so many treasures in each eye-boggling illustration, each described down to the tiniest detail.

Now turn to page 40 and test your memory. Can you remember where you saw each item? If not, don't worry, we won't hang you from the yardarm . . . just yet! Grab your magnifying glass and go back for one more swashbuckling search-and-find adventure. You're bound to spot much more this time around.

Lastly, take a look at the gallery of more pirate rogues on page 38 before turning to page 44 to learn how to "Talk Like a Pirate." Well! What are you waiting for, you crusty ol' seadog? Hoist the mainsail and set sail for the journey of a lifetime!

CONTENTS

IN THE TIME OF PIRATES

The explorer Christopher Columbus reached the Americas in 1492, claiming these lands for the Spanish king. From then on, the Spanish sent large ships, called galleons, to bring back gold, silver, and gems across the Atlantic, making rich pickings for thieves. And so the Golden Age of Piracy began. And the place to find these pirates was Port Royal in Jamaica: the center of Caribbean trade, famed for its raiders, smugglers, and mischief-makers.

Privateers were also found in Port Royal. These were sailors who were allowed by their governments to attack enemy ships. They were supposed to share their booty with the government, but many privateers became greedy, keeping their ill-gotten gains for themselves. You got all sorts in Port Royal!

10 THINGS TO SPOT

PIRATE Pirates usually worked in small gangs. They attacked other ships, hoping to defeat the crew and steal their cargo.

PRIVATEER Privateers owned their own ships and had a special license to attack enemy ships.

BUCCANEER Buccaneers were pirates too, who often joined forces to make large gangs. These gangs raided coastal towns and villages in the Caribbean.

TREASURE Pirate treasure was divided among the crew, with a double share for the captain.

CROW'S NEST This platform is where you'll find the ship's lookout: a sailor who could climb the tallest mast to watch for ships.

DEATH IN PORT ROYAL Seafaring was a dangerous business, with a high risk of illness or injury, so funerals happened often in Port Royal.

CHURCH Many of Port Royal's churches were turned into drinking halls for thirsty pirates.

COINS Lots of coins would have changed hands here, including "pieces of eight" (silver Spanish coins) and gold doubloons.

FRESH FOOD Fresh vegetables and fruit were rare on board a ship, so sailors would have sought these out when in port.

GOODS Port Royal was a hub for the trade of many goods, including sugar and cotton.

A PIRATE'S SHIP

The most practical ship for pirates was called a sloop. These were much smaller than warships, with one main mast, and were designed to be fast and nimble. Sloops could be fitted with cannons, making them perfect for attacking enemy ships. They had shallow hulls, meaning they could sail close to the shore, hiding out in shallow bays and inlets where larger naval ships could not follow.

Mast

Topsail

Flying jib

Mainsail

Jib

Stern

Main staysail

Bow

Hull

Barley

Beads

Wine

Wheat

Tools

Porcelain

Beer

Cardamom

Cotton

Turpentine

Pepper

Tobacco

Cedar

Chocolate

Cinnamon

Cloves

Salt Fish

Coffee

Coins

MERCHANTS ON THE HIGH SEAS

Pirates didn't steal only gold, silver, and gems—they were also on the lookout for lots of other valuables. From the 16th century onward, merchants began shipping precious cargoes all over the world, so there were plenty of opportunities for pirates to plunder their ships.

The value of some of these goods may seem surprising. While gold and silver have always been prized, spices such as nutmeg, mace, and even pepper were more valuable at one time. These grew wild on islands in the Pacific Ocean, but because of their rarity in Europe, they could be brought back and sold for huge sums of money.

Copper

Corn

Farm tools

Gemstones and precious jewels

Gold

Salt

Wool

Ebony

Flax

Olive oil

Furniture

Ginger

Tea

Silk thread and cloth

Slaves

Sake

Tin

Smoked Fish

Skins and furs

10 THINGS TO SPOT

Can you find these traded goods in the market scene below?

 BEER Water stored in barrels quickly became undrinkable at sea, so beer was a popular alternative—and safe—during long journeys.

 SILVER Precious metals were traded widely, and were used to make coins, jewelry, and luxury items for the rich.

 SUGAR Enormously popular in Europe, sugar from the Caribbean was soon one of the world's most valuable crops.

 SILK THREAD & CLOTH Originally produced in China, this luxurious and colorful material attracted very high prices in Europe.

 PORCELAIN Portuguese and Dutch merchants helped to make Chinese and Japanese designs fashionable in Europe.

 SALT FISH Salting and drying fish stopped it from going bad. This way, it could be transported long distances from one country to another.

 IVORY Expertly carved by artists and craftsmen, ivory was used to make jewelry, works of art, piano keys, and luxury goods.

 GEMSTONES & JEWELS Since the earliest times, diamonds and colored gems have been eagerly sought by the rich and powerful.

 GUNS & OTHER WEAPONS Pirates used weapons, but traded them, too. They were often sold at ports or to crews of other vessels.

 TOBACCO First grown in the Americas, this plant became a valuable item when European settlers started smoking it.

A tiny bag of spices from Indonesia could make a man rich for life. Because of this, merchants were in constant danger of attack as they sailed back to European shores. Which valuable goods can you spot in this picture?

Rum

Sugar

Rice

Silver

Hemp for rope

Pottery

Ivory

Knives

Guns and other weapons

Pitch

Indigo (dye)

Mahogany

Metal trinkets

Nutmeg

10 THINGS TO SPOT

Use your magnifying glass to find where these spices, food, and other valuable goods came from. What else can you spot on the map?

PEPPER (India) This seasoning was highly prized by wealthy Europeans who used it to flavor food.

CEDAR, CLOVES, AND CINNAMON (Sri Lanka) Traders grew rich from carrying fragrant spices like these to Europe.

GOLD (Central Africa) Everyone wanted gold, which could be used to make jewelry and other luxury items.

OLIVE OIL (Mediterranean) For centuries, olive oil has been used across the world in cooking, medicine, and religious rituals.

NAVIGATING THE SEVEN SEAS

Not only were pirates some of history's toughest adventurers—they were also some of the most skillful. Crossing thousands of miles of ocean was dangerous, and every crew depended heavily on the ship's navigator. The captain would decide where to go, and the navigator would plan the route on maps known as charts. He used sophisticated instruments to figure out the ship's location from the position of the sun and stars.

Even in good weather, crossing the Atlantic could take three months or more. Pirates also sailed around the coast of Africa to reach India, and from North America down toward Mexico and the Caribbean. Books of charts called "waggoners" showed them trade routes so they could track down merchant ships.

A NAVIGATOR'S TOOLBOX

The navigator would figure out his ship's location by measuring the latitude (the position north or south of the equator) and the longitude (the east-west position). To figure out the latitude, he used a tool called a backstaff to measure the angle of the sun at noon each day. To figure out the longitude, the navigator had to rely on an estimate of the ship's speed over a period of time. Because of this, it was important to know the time, but clocks were rare and expensive, so many pirates used an hourglass full of salt or sand.

TELESCOPE Pirates used these to look for landmarks, which helped plot a ship's position, and also to spot enemy vessels.

WAGGONER This was a large book of sea charts, which showed shipping routes and coastlines.

ANIMAL FURS (Russia) Seal furs and sealskins, used to make clothing, were popular for trading.

 CORN (Mexico) Corn has been grown in Mexico for more than 4,000 years, and was an important trade item.

SALT (Eastern Europe) For centuries, salt has been a valuable substance: humans need it to live—and to flavor our food!

 RUM (Jamaica) Yo-ho-ho, and a bottle of rum! This favorite seafarer's drink is made by fermenting the juice from sugarcane.

 RICE (China) One of China's most important crops, rice was shipped overseas in huge quantities.

 TEA (China) The Chinese have been drinking tea for thousands of years, and it became popular in Europe in the 17th century.

COMPASS Sailors sometimes made their own compasses by stroking a nail with a piece of magnetic rock, then floating it in some water.

BACKSTAFF The navigator used this instrument to measure the angle of the sun, to figure out the ship's latitude.

SEXTANT This tool, invented later than the backstaff, was also used to figure out latitude, but could be used at night as well as in the day.

SHIP'S CHRONOMETER This was a special kind of clock, for use at sea, which helped sailors figure out their longitude.

LIFE ON BOARD

Life on board a pirate ship was hard. The crew had to obey a set of rules called the Pirate Code. Stealing from each other, fighting, and cheating at cards were banned, and obedience to the captain was crucial. In return, each pirate received his fair share of any treasure the crew captured.

Long voyages were difficult for all sailors, not just pirates. Water became undrinkable within days of leaving port, so the crew had to drink beer. Meals were mostly salt pork and dry biscuits known as "hardtack," which were often crawling with maggots. Chickens were sometimes kept to provide fresh eggs and meat. Pirates sometimes managed to catch fish or dolphins to eat. Slow-moving turtles were easy to keep alive on deck.

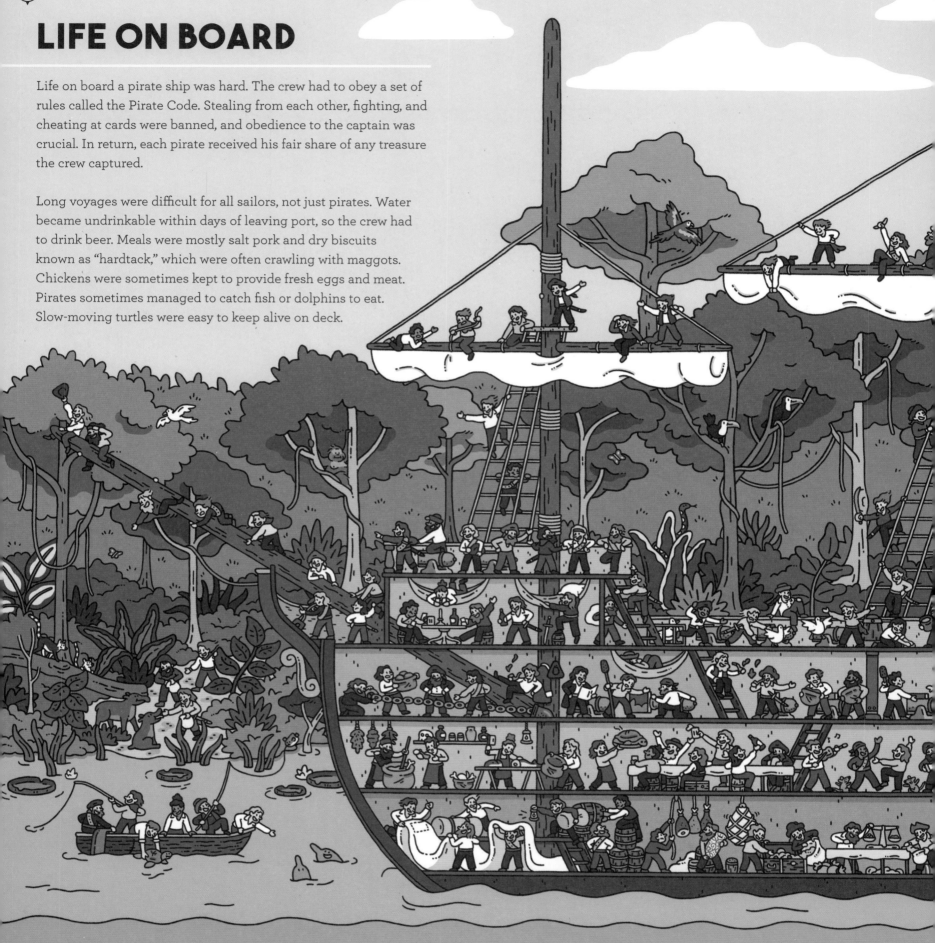

10 THINGS TO SPOT

Use your magnifying glass to spot these items on board. What else can you see in the picture?

 SHIP'S COOK When supplies ran low, the ship's cook made soup by boiling bones—or even leather—in a cauldron.

 CARPENTER The carpenter worked hard to keep the ship's hull strong and watertight. He repaired any broken masts and the barrels used to store food, beer, and water.

 SURGERY Unless pirates had been able to kidnap an experienced surgeon, the carpenter also had to operate on injured crewmates. He would have used his woodworking tools, with no anesthetic for the patient!

 MASTER GUNNER The master gunner made sure the guns and cannons were in working order.

Some ships carried stocks of limes, but these rotted or soon ran out on long voyages. Without fruit or vegetables, many pirates became ill with a disease called scurvy. When this happened, they would turn yellow and their hair and teeth could fall out!

 POWDER MONKEY A boy known as the "powder monkey" carried gunpowder to the cannons during attacks on other ships.

 BOATSWAIN The boatswain was in charge of the ship's maintenance, and supervised the raising of the anchor and the handling of sails.

 BROKEN SAILS If sails were damaged in a storm, the sailmaker would repair them.

 QUARTERMASTER The quartermaster managed the ship's supplies and kept order, making sure the crew kept to the Pirate Code. Any rule-breakers would be flogged.

 SWAB Pirates known as swabs or swabbies had to keep the decks clean and repaired. The decks were scrubbed daily with salt water to prevent the timbers splitting in the sun.

FISHING Catching fish and turtles was one way for the pirates to enjoy a fresh meal.

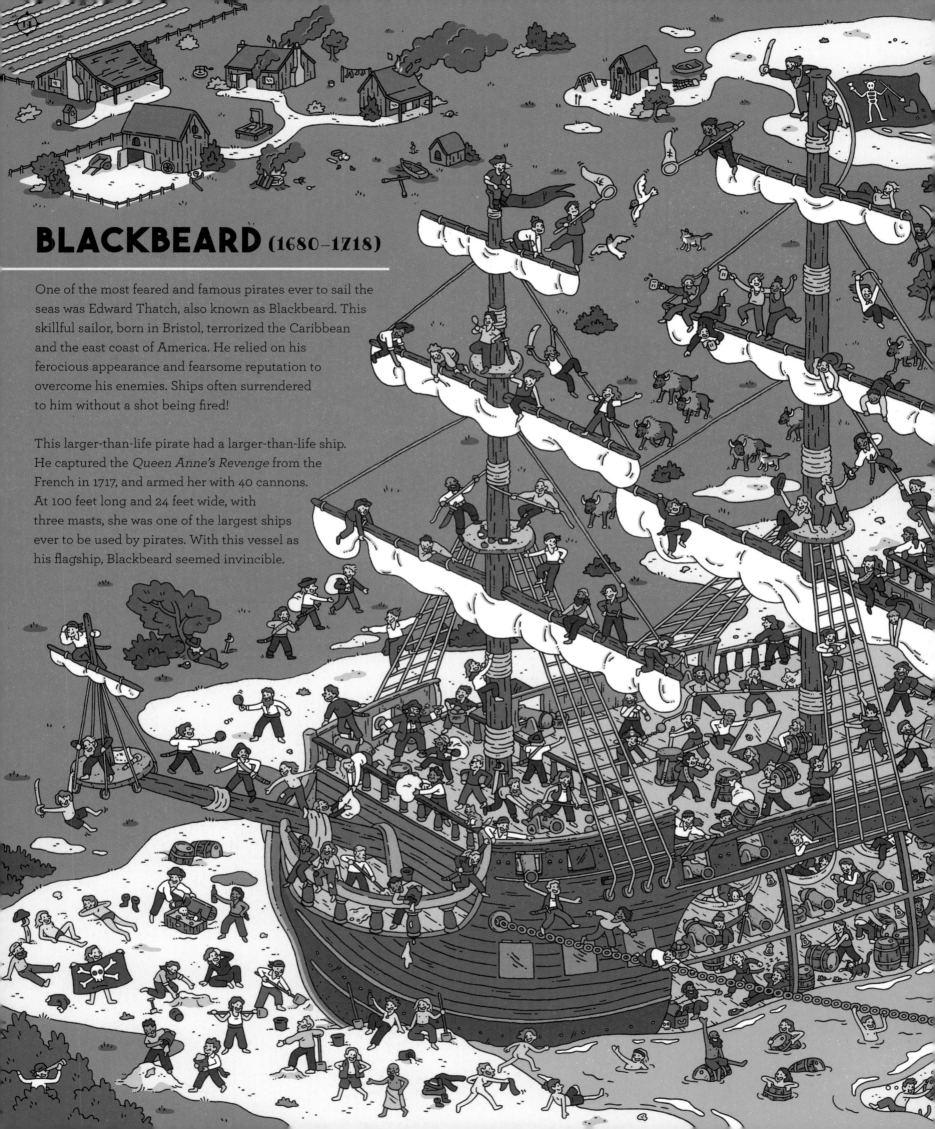

BLACKBEARD (1680–1718)

One of the most feared and famous pirates ever to sail the seas was Edward Thatch, also known as Blackbeard. This skillful sailor, born in Bristol, terrorized the Caribbean and the east coast of America. He relied on his ferocious appearance and fearsome reputation to overcome his enemies. Ships often surrendered to him without a shot being fired!

This larger-than-life pirate had a larger-than-life ship. He captured the *Queen Anne's Revenge* from the French in 1717, and armed her with 40 cannons. At 100 feet long and 24 feet wide, with three masts, she was one of the largest ships ever to be used by pirates. With this vessel as his flagship, Blackbeard seemed invincible.

10 THINGS TO SPOT

BLACKBEARD Before a battle, Blackbeard would tie smoking fuses into his hair and beard to make himself look more frightening.

CANNON The *Queen Anne's Revenge* was well armed with 40 captured cannons. Can you spot this one?

CAPTAIN'S QUARTERS Located at the stern (back) of the ship, this was the place to sit out the worst of the weather—or a mutiny!

BLACKBEARD'S FLAG The skeleton on Blackbeard's flag was shown stabbing a heart and holding an hourglass, to signify that your time was running out!

SAILOR Many of Blackbeard's crew were escaped slaves.

WATER BARREL Supplies of fresh water were kept in the hold at the bottom of the ship, along with the other supplies and cargo.

ANCHOR The anchor weighed about 2,800 pounds (the same as three grand pianos) and could take up to an hour to raise.

PRISONER Blackbeard was known for taking hostages, demanding a sizeable ransom for their release.

CAT Mice and rats could bring diseases on ship, so cats were often kept on board to keep vermin at bay.

BISON AND WOLVES Wildlife in North Carolina included bison and timber wolves—both were later hunted to extinction.

The *Queen Anne's Revenge* met her match when she ran aground in the shallow shores of a North Carolina inlet in June 1718. The badly damaged ship had to be abandoned, and Blackbeard and his crew fled in smaller ships. A few months later, Blackbeard was killed in battle with a British naval captain.

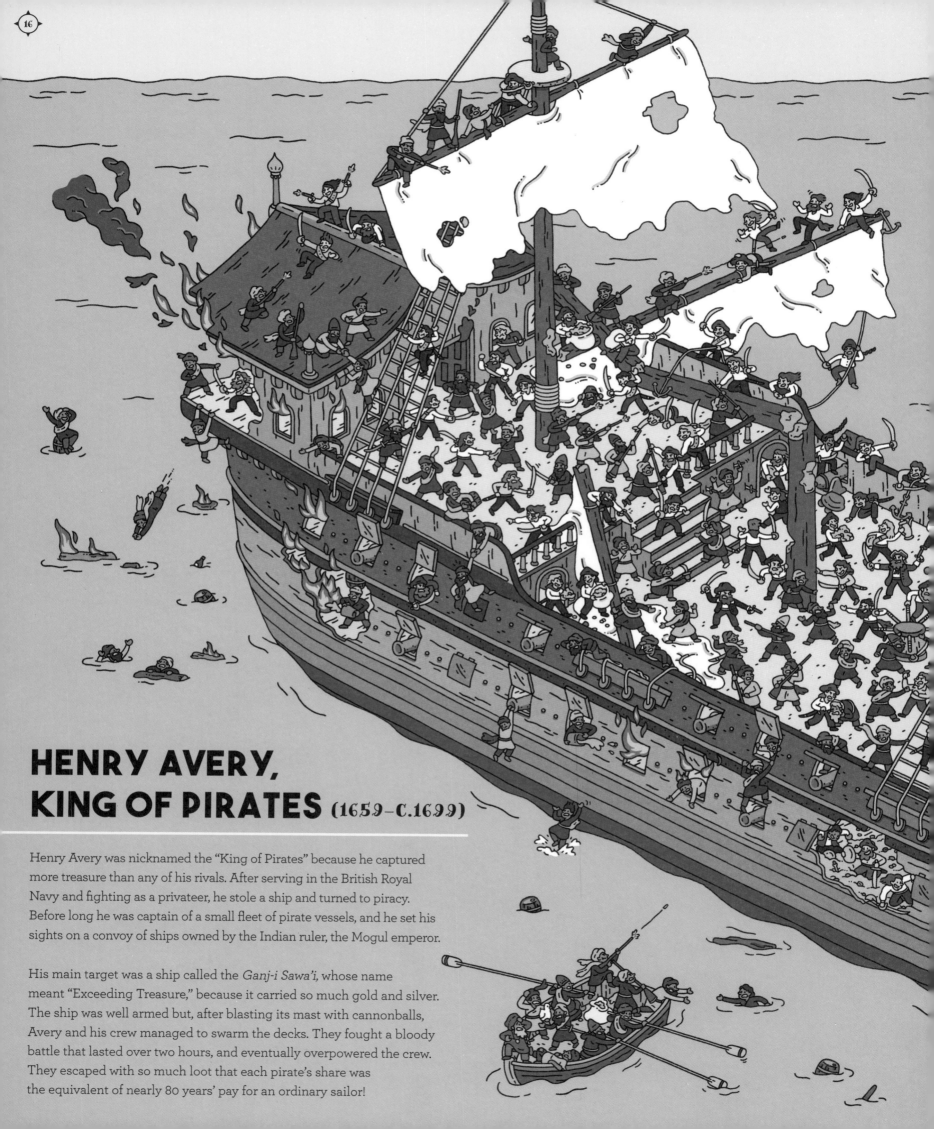

HENRY AVERY, KING OF PIRATES (1659–C.1699)

Henry Avery was nicknamed the "King of Pirates" because he captured more treasure than any of his rivals. After serving in the British Royal Navy and fighting as a privateer, he stole a ship and turned to piracy. Before long he was captain of a small fleet of pirate vessels, and he set his sights on a convoy of ships owned by the Indian ruler, the Mogul emperor.

His main target was a ship called the *Ganj-i Sawa'i,* whose name meant "Exceeding Treasure," because it carried so much gold and silver. The ship was well armed but, after blasting its mast with cannonballs, Avery and his crew managed to swarm the decks. They fought a bloody battle that lasted over two hours, and eventually overpowered the crew. They escaped with so much loot that each pirate's share was the equivalent of nearly 80 years' pay for an ordinary sailor!

10 THINGS TO SPOT

LUCKY PIRATE Avery is best known for being one of the few pirate captains to retire with his loot without being arrested or killed.

ROPES AND HOOKS Avery's crew used ropes and hooks called grappling irons to clamber on board the Mogul emperor's ship.

MUSKETS The *Ganj-i Sawa'i* had 400 men armed with long-barreled guns, called muskets. But these weren't enough to defeat the pirates.

CANNONS The emperor's ship had more cannons than the pirates' ship, but one of these exploded early in the battle, killing the gunners and causing chaos among the crew.

PISTOLS AND CUTLASSES The pirates were armed with pistols and cutlasses: short, curved swords perfect for slashing ropes and for use in combat on a crowded deck.

FLAG It is thought that Avery's flag was red with four gold chevrons, symbolizing danger.

TREASURE While the battle raged on, several pirates began searching the decks for the famous treasure hoard.

CAPTAIN OF THE *GANJ-I SAWA'I* In the confusion, the captain of the *Ganj-i Sawa'i* abandoned his crew instead of fighting.

EMPEROR'S DAUGHTER Legend has it that during the battle, Avery captured the emperor's daughter, who was traveling back from a pilgrimage.

ABANDON SHIP! Many of the passengers of the *Ganj-i Sawa'i* tried to escape from Avery's bloodthirsty crew by jumping overboard.

10 THINGS TO SPOT

 BLACK BART Like many pirate captains, Black Bart was stylish as well as bold. Dressed in a crimson waistcoat and breeches, he often wore a red feather in his hat and a gold chain around his neck with a large diamond cross.

 JUMPING SHIP When Black Bart's sloop, *The Fortune*, was seen approaching Trepassey, many sailors abandoned their ships and ran to hide in the town.

 DANGEROUS WATERS The waters around Trepassey were very dangerous. There were many shipwrecks in the area, as vessels often ran around or got caught in storms.

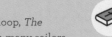 **NEW RECRUITS** When Black Bart's pirate crew recruited sailors to join them, the sailors had to swear on the Bible that they would obey the Pirate Code.

BLACK BART (1682–1722)

While working on a slave ship off the coast of West Africa, the Welsh sailor Bartholomew Roberts was captured by pirates. The captain and his crew were impressed by Roberts's skill as a navigator, and persuaded him that he could earn more money as a pirate. When the captain was killed during a raid, the ship's crew elected Roberts as their new leader.

He renamed himself "Black Bart" and went on to attack and loot more than 400 ships: more than any other pirate at the time. He was very daring. Most pirates avoided towns and ports for fear of being caught, but Black Bart often ordered his crew to sail right into harbor. In 1720, he attacked the port of Trepassey in Newfoundland and captured all the ships without firing a shot.

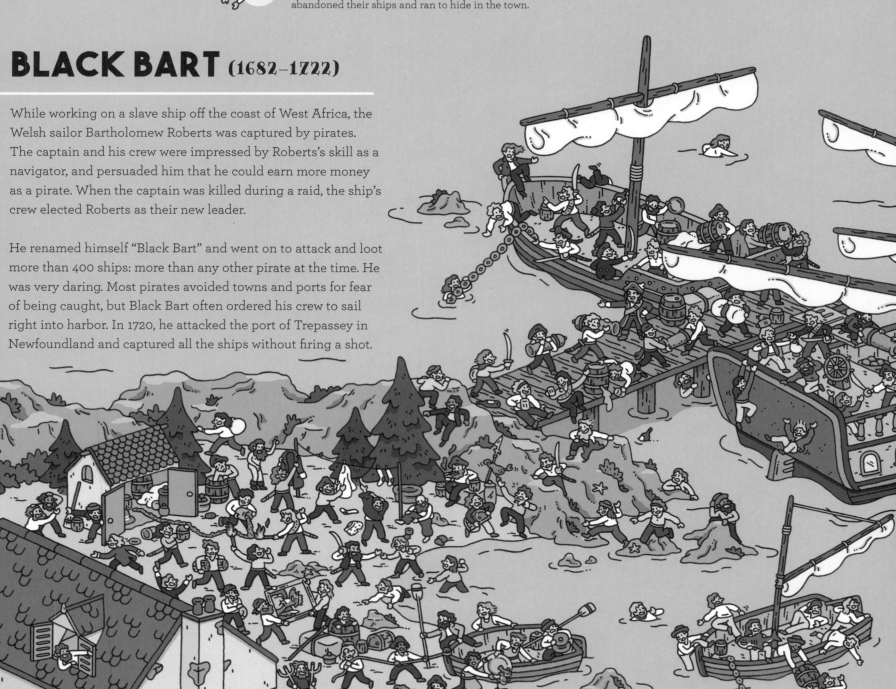

CREW Many of Black Bart's crew members were former slaves from Africa.

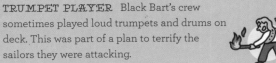 **TRUMPET PLAYER** Black Bart's crew sometimes played loud trumpets and drums on deck. This was part of a plan to terrify the sailors they were attacking.

FLAG Black Bart hated the governors of Barbados and Martinique. His flag showed a pirate standing on top of two skulls.

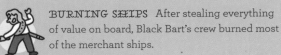 **BURNING SHIPS** After stealing everything of value on board, Black Bart's crew burned most of the merchant ships.

 CANNON CARRIER Black Bart kept one of the ships from Trepassey: a two-masted brig, which he fitted with 16 cannons.

TEA DRINKER Black Bart liked to drink tea, but his crew often stole barrels of beer and rum from their victims.

When Black Bart sailed into Trepassey harbor in June 1720, he seized 22 merchant ships and 150 fishing vessels. He was said to have been angry with the ships' captains for not putting up more of a fight.

ANNE BONNY (1700–C.1782)
AND MARY READ (1690–1721)

18th-century sailors were often superstitious, and some believed that it was bad luck to have a lady aboard a ship. This didn't stop a number of brave women disguising themselves as men and taking to the waters. The most famous was an Irish pirate named Anne Bonny, who sailed around the Caribbean on a sloop, *The William*. During her travels, she met another woman pirate, Mary Read, and the two joined forces.

Dressed in men's clothes, the two friends were more than a match for enemies they met during their travels. Mary is said to have saved the life of a pirate she fell in love with by defending him with her cutlass from another crew member. And when *The William* came under attack from the Royal Navy, Anne fought on fiercely while shouting at her cowardly shipmates to come out from their hiding places to fight.

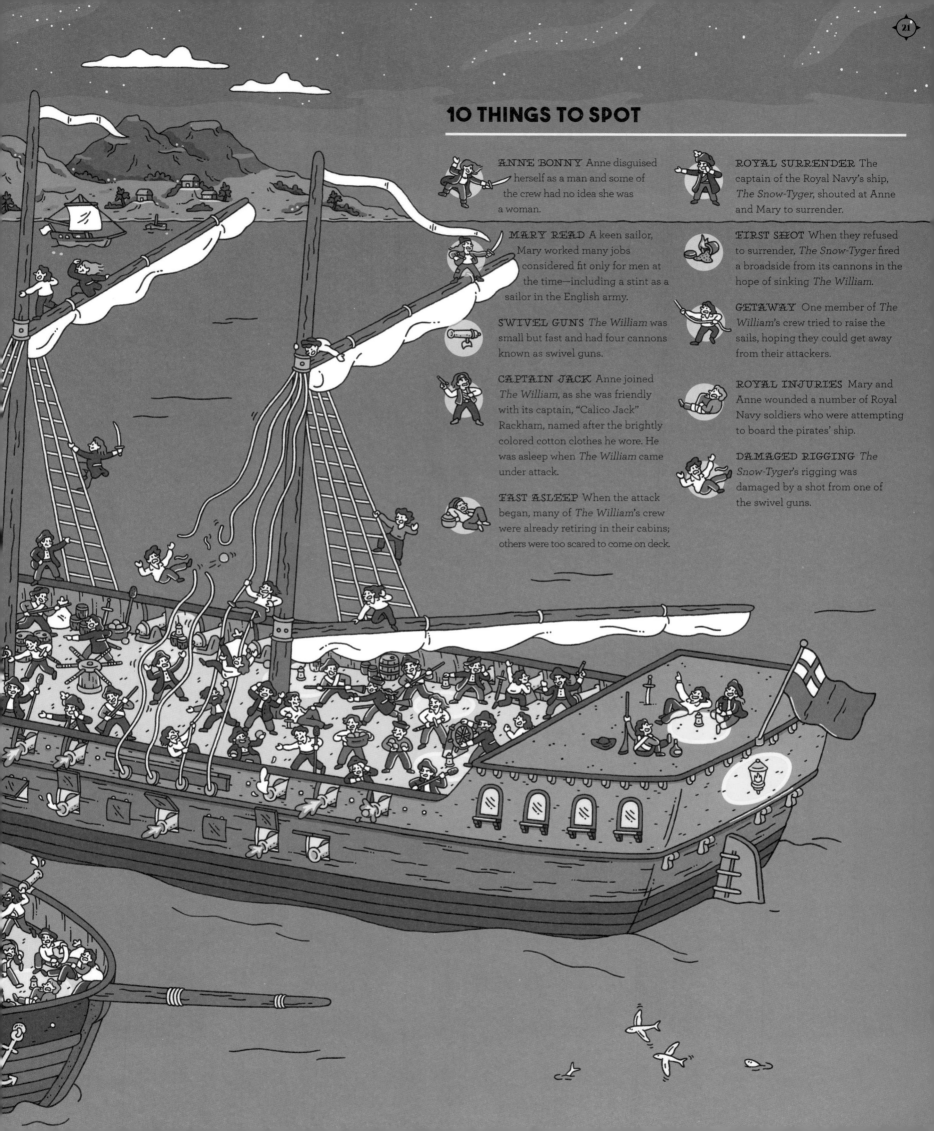

10 THINGS TO SPOT

ANNE BONNY Anne disguised herself as a man and some of the crew had no idea she was a woman.

MARY READ A keen sailor, Mary worked many jobs considered fit only for men at the time—including a stint as a sailor in the English army.

SWIVEL GUNS *The William* was small but fast and had four cannons known as swivel guns.

CAPTAIN JACK Anne joined *The William*, as she was friendly with its captain, "Calico Jack" Rackham, named after the brightly colored cotton clothes he wore. He was asleep when *The William* came under attack.

FAST ASLEEP When the attack began, many of *The William*'s crew were already retiring in their cabins; others were too scared to come on deck.

ROYAL SURRENDER The captain of the Royal Navy's ship, *The Snow-Tyger*, shouted at Anne and Mary to surrender.

FIRST SHOT When they refused to surrender, *The Snow-Tyger* fired a broadside from its cannons in the hope of sinking *The William*.

GETAWAY One member of *The William*'s crew tried to raise the sails, hoping they could get away from their attackers.

ROYAL INJURIES Mary and Anne wounded a number of Royal Navy soldiers who were attempting to board the pirates' ship.

DAMAGED RIGGING *The Snow-Tyger*'s rigging was damaged by a shot from one of the swivel guns.

BLACK CAESAR (1690–1718)

The pirate way of life was popular not only with privateers and buccaneers, but with slave traders and escaped slaves, too. The most dashing of these was an African pirate named Black Caesar, who joined Blackbeard's crew on the *Queen Anne's Revenge*.

For a while he was captain of his own ship and sailed around the islands of the Florida Keys looking for ships to plunder. Tall and cunning, Caesar's favorite trick was to approach his potential target in a smaller boat, called a longboat, with some of his men disguised as shipwrecked sailors asking for help.

When a larger vessel came to their rescue, Black Caesar would bring out their guns and demand supplies and ammunition, threatening to sink the ship if they were refused. Then they would climb on board and overcome their rescuers, stealing whatever they could find on the ship.

10 THINGS TO SPOT

 BLACK CAESAR Known for his huge size and immense strength, Caesar was an African tribal warrior before he was taken as a slave.

OARS The longboat he used to trick his victims had oars rather than sails. Usually this sort of boat was used to row to the shoreline when the water was too shallow for a larger vessel to sail in.

 HIDDEN AMMUNITION While pretending they were shipwrecked sailors, Caesar and his crew concealed small weapons such as daggers and flintlock pistols in their clothes.

 FULL HOARD As well as treasure, Caesar's crew stole ammunition and supplies, including any food or beer they found on board.

To avoid being caught when they were close to shore, Caesar would take down his mast before partly submerging his ship in shallow water, using ropes attached to rocks. The crew would then hide in a nearby swamp until it was safe to go back and refloat the ship.

ALL ABOARD Their victims would help the pirates climb onto their own ships. By the time they realized what they had done, it was too late to escape.

BLACK PIRATES There were many other black pirates besides Caesar. They were treated the same as other pirates and so had far more freedom than if they remained slaves.

PRISONERS Sometimes Caesar would also take prisoners, who were kept on a small, uninhabited island where Caesar had his secret camp.

HIDING PLACE Caesar liked the Florida Keys because he could hide with his pirates in the many small inlets that were too shallow for larger ships to explore.

KEEPING WATCH Once Caesar's crew had partly sunk the ship, they took turns keeping watch on a nearby island for pirate hunters.

SILVER LOOT On an average raid, it is thought that Caesar collected about twenty solid silver bars or ingots.

CAPTAIN WILLIAM KIDD (1645–1701)

William Kidd was a Scottish privateer who became a pirate during his travels around the Indian Ocean. His greatest prize was the *Quedagh Merchant*—a large ship known for its ability to carry heavy, valuable loads—which he spotted off the Indian coast. Kidd's own vessel, *Adventure Galley*, had oars as well as square-rigged sails, which meant that he was quick to attack when there was no wind. Using the oars, his crew was able to pull up alongside the *Quedagh Merchant*.

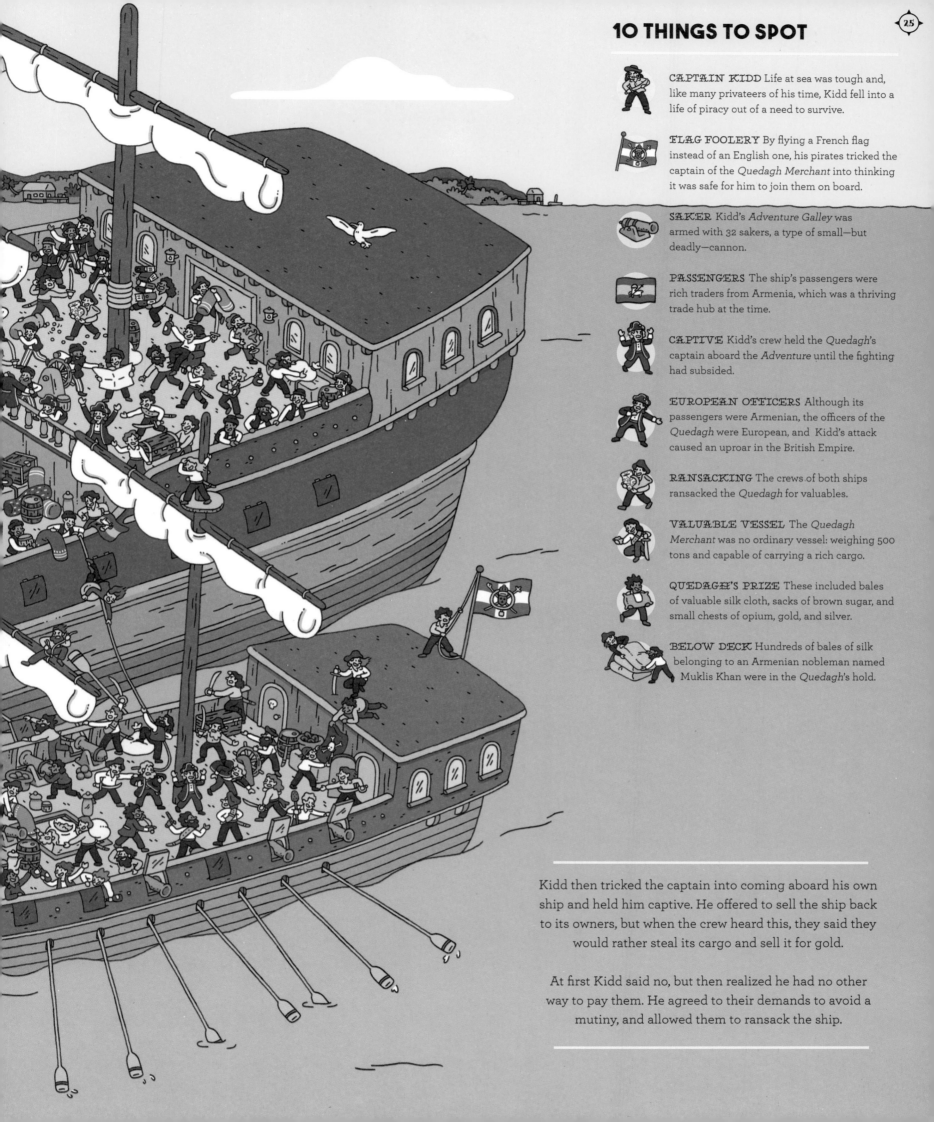

10 THINGS TO SPOT

CAPTAIN KIDD Life at sea was tough and, like many privateers of his time, Kidd fell into a life of piracy out of a need to survive.

FLAG FOOLERY By flying a French flag instead of an English one, his pirates tricked the captain of the *Quedagh Merchant* into thinking it was safe for him to join them on board.

SAKER Kidd's *Adventure Galley* was armed with 32 sakers, a type of small—but deadly—cannon.

PASSENGERS The ship's passengers were rich traders from Armenia, which was a thriving trade hub at the time.

CAPTIVE Kidd's crew held the *Quedagh's* captain aboard the *Adventure* until the fighting had subsided.

EUROPEAN OFFICERS Although its passengers were Armenian, the officers of the *Quedagh* were European, and Kidd's attack caused an uproar in the British Empire.

RANSACKING The crews of both ships ransacked the *Quedagh* for valuables.

VALUABLE VESSEL The *Quedagh Merchant* was no ordinary vessel: weighing 500 tons and capable of carrying a rich cargo.

QUEDAGH'S PRIZE These included bales of valuable silk cloth, sacks of brown sugar, and small chests of opium, gold, and silver.

BELOW DECK Hundreds of bales of silk belonging to an Armenian nobleman named Muklis Khan were in the *Quedagh's* hold.

Kidd then tricked the captain into coming aboard his own ship and held him captive. He offered to sell the ship back to its owners, but when the crew heard this, they said they would rather steal its cargo and sell it for gold.

At first Kidd said no, but then realized he had no other way to pay them. He agreed to their demands to avoid a mutiny, and allowed them to ransack the ship.

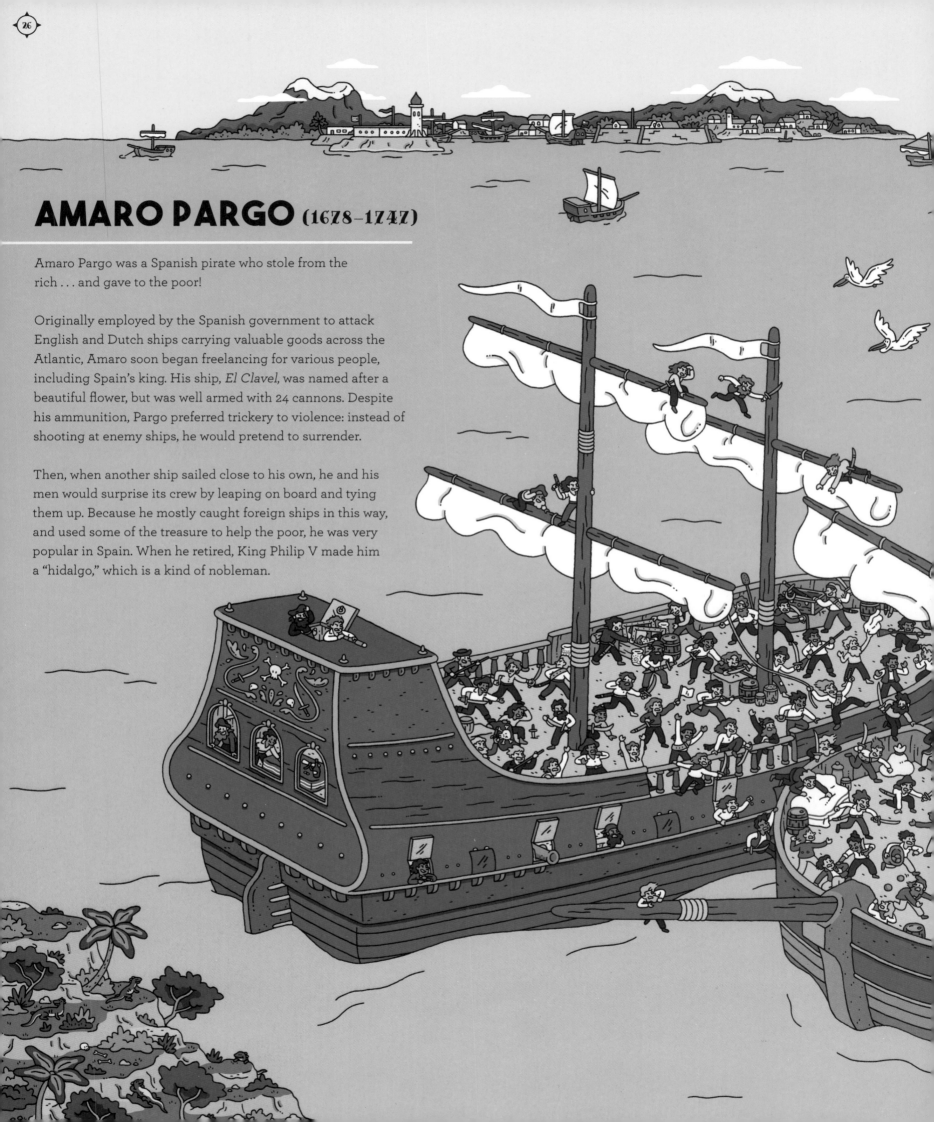

AMARO PARGO (1678–1747)

Amaro Pargo was a Spanish pirate who stole from the rich . . . and gave to the poor!

Originally employed by the Spanish government to attack English and Dutch ships carrying valuable goods across the Atlantic, Amaro soon began freelancing for various people, including Spain's king. His ship, *El Clavel*, was named after a beautiful flower, but was well armed with 24 cannons. Despite his ammunition, Pargo preferred trickery to violence: instead of shooting at enemy ships, he would pretend to surrender.

Then, when another ship sailed close to his own, he and his men would surprise its crew by leaping on board and tying them up. Because he mostly caught foreign ships in this way, and used some of the treasure to help the poor, he was very popular in Spain. When he retired, King Philip V made him a "hidalgo," which is a kind of nobleman.

10 THINGS TO SPOT

 AMARO PARGO Many pirates were huge and strong but Pargo looked pale and skinny. He was a religious man and sometimes wore a cross studded with diamonds.

 FLAG His personal emblem was a winking skull on two crossed bones.

 FINE CHINA A chest on board *El Clavel* contained Pargo's collection of rare Chinese porcelain and valuable paintings that he had looted from enemy vessels.

 PRISONER Pargo found a priest among those being held prisoner, and is known to have spent some time with him discussing questions about the Bible.

 SURRENDER Waving a white flag of surrender tricked other captains into sailing closer to Pargo's ship.

 ON BOARD When close enough to board, Amaro and his crew would leap onto the other vessel before pulling out their weapons.

SABER Amaro's crew were known for a kind of wide-bladed sword called a saber.

 ROYAL CALLING An official document kept on board showed that Pargo was working for the Spanish king. This was known as a "letter of marque."

 WINE CASKS Pargo owned several vineyards on the Spanish island of Tenerife and made his own wine, which was carried in barrels to sell on the other side of the Atlantic.

 HEAVY LOAD Pargo could tell when his victims were carrying lots of gold and silver because the extra weight meant their ship sat low in the water.

10 THINGS TO SPOT

NAUGHTY NAVY Olivier Levasseur began his career in the French navy, but got a taste for piracy and refused to return to France when he was ordered back from war.

ANCHOR AWAY! It was listing badly, meaning 'leaning over'. Only a heavy anchor and chain prevented it from drifting out to sea.

CANNONS OVERBOARD! In the hope of saving it, the crew hauled all 72 cannons on deck and then pushed them overboard.

MENDING THE PLANKS Some of their companions were working on the outside of the hull, repairing sections of planking smashed by the storm.

OLIVIER LEVASSEUR (1690–1730)

Olivier Levasseur was a French pirate who wore an eye patch after losing an eye in a fight. His nickname, "The Buzzard," described the way he swooped down on his victims like a deadly bird of prey.

As a member of various pirate gangs, he captured several vessels and burned down a fortress on the west coast of Africa. Then, as captain of his own ship, he sailed around Mozambique attacking anyone crossing the Indian Ocean.

His most successful raid was on the *Nossa Senhora do Cabo*, a great Portuguese warship carrying treasure from Goa, in India, to Portugal. He first spotted the ship anchored off the island of Réunion after it had been badly damaged in a storm.

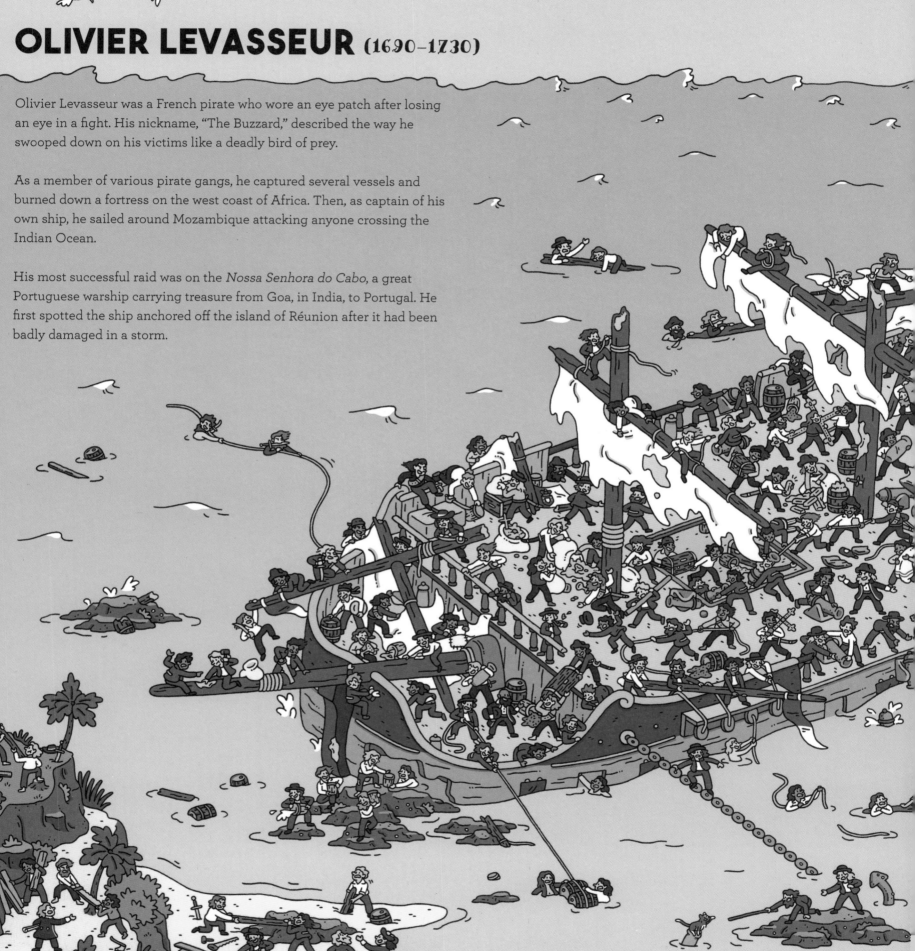

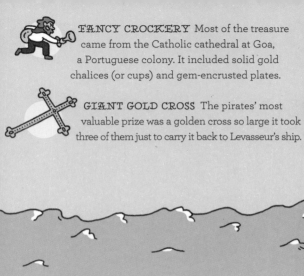

FANCY CROCKERY Most of the treasure came from the Catholic cathedral at Goa, a Portuguese colony. It included solid gold chalices (or cups) and gem-encrusted plates.

GIANT GOLD CROSS The pirates' most valuable prize was a golden cross so large it took three of them just to carry it back to Levasseur's ship.

TREASURE CHESTS As well as bars of pure gold and silver, the thieves found wooden chests full of pearls and diamonds.

BISHOP'S ROBES There was so much treasure that only the richest passengers were robbed—the bishop of Goa was ordered to hand over his lavish robes of silk and gold thread.

PORTUGUESE FLAG The Portuguese flag at the time was different from the modern one and included a scarlet-and-gold crown.

SECRET CODE Levasseur liked to bury his treasure in a place only he knew. He recorded the location using a secret code, which no one has managed to crack after nearly 300 years.

With the crew hard at work in a desperate attempt to stop the ship sinking, Levasseur and his pirates didn't need to use their weapons. They just clambered up the other side of the hull and began stealing everything they could find.

STENKA RAZIN (1630–1671)

Stepan Timofeyevich Razin, known as Stenka Razin, was a Cossack warrior who became a pirate and hid out in the marshes around the town of Panshinskoye, Russia. Fighting the tsar and the ruthless noblemen who ruled Russia made him a popular person in Russian folklore.

As his gang of pirates grew stronger, he began raiding coastal towns and villages, stealing a great convoy of barges belonging to the wealthy merchants of Moscow. Using these as his personal battle fleet, he sailed up the Volga River attacking and burning important government forts on both banks.

10 THINGS TO SPOT

FIERY SIGN Once the guards had been overpowered, Razin signaled to his men waiting outside with a flaming torch. Lit torches were usually used to find your way through the city streets after dark.

CHRISTIAN MONKS Disguised in long robes with hoods, Razin's men looked like ordinary monks visiting the church.

RELIGIOUS DOMES Most churches in Russia at this time had towers topped by distinctive onion-shaped domes.

AMBUSH CREW The rest of Razin's men came up the Yaik River in long rowing boats. Hidden from view, they waited silently for the gates to open.

SLEEP TIGHT The huge gates were shut each night and guarded by armed men.

BAR THE WAY A thick wood-and-iron bar had to be removed before the gates could be opened.

ARMED FORCES The people of Yaitsk surrendered immediately, but armed soldiers soon appeared outside the walls.

SWITCHING SIDES Some of these troops decided to join Razin. A pirate's life seemed much more appealing than a soldier's life.

FUR HATS Cossacks like Razin came from some of the coldest regions of Russia and often wore distinctive animal fur hats.

CURVED SWORDS Their favorite weapon was the shashka, a long, curved sword.

He had a brilliant plan to capture the walled city of Yaitsk, which was heavily defended. Razin and 40 of his men disguised themselves as religious pilgrims. They looked like they had come to pray at the church. Once inside the walls, they opened the tall wooden gates so that more pirates could rush in. Because they robbed only the rich, and left the poor alone, the soldiers sent to recapture Yaitsk refused to fight the pirates.

JAMES FORD (1775–1833)

James Ford looked like an ordinary, law-abiding American businessman, but after dark he turned to piracy with his notorious Ferry Gang. Unlike other pirates, this pirate crew didn't head out to sea, though, preferring to hijack flatboats and barges on the Ohio River.

They were based in a place called Cave-in-Rock, which had a long history of highwaymen and piracy. The spacious, dark cave that gave its name to the area made the perfect hideout for Ford and his pirate gang.

The narrow entrance was well hidden and difficult to spot from the outside, but it gave the pirates inside a clear view of who and what was coming down the river. When the Ohio flooded, it may even have been possible for them to paddle their canoes right into the cave.

10 THINGS TO SPOT

JUDGEMENT DAY James Ford condemned criminals by day, and was secretly the leader of "Ford's Ferry Gang" by night.

SLOW BOATS Flatboats or 'scows' were ideal for hauling goods down wide, shallow rivers like the Ohio, but they were slow and hard to manoeuvre, making them easy prey for pirates.

HEAVY STEERING A long steering oar was used to keep the boat in midstream so it wouldn't run aground. This was heavy and required two men to operate it.

LONG WALK HOME At the end of each trip, the exhausted crew would have to walk many miles back along the river because the boats were usually broken up and sold for timber once they reached their destination.

As the local judge and sheriff, Ford was well placed to keep his men from being caught and, for years, the Ferry Gang effectively ruled this stretch of river.

DEADLY SURPRISE Spotting a vessel coming downriver from their concealed hideout, the pirates would row up to it before pulling out their revolvers and threatening the crew.

GUN HOLES Crews sometimes fired back with rifles. Some flatboats had small slit windows for this, like an old-fashioned castle.

PIRATE PLUNDER If they managed to board the vessel, the pirates stole anything they thought they could sell. This could include captured slaves, as well as barrels of whiskey and other goods.

TAKEOUT Crews cooked and ate their meals outdoors on the deck of the boat, as each journey could take up to six weeks.

LURKING SHARKS If one of the boatmen jumped into the water to escape, he had to hope he didn't meet one of the ferocious bull sharks that sometimes hunted in the river.

OLD WRECKS After being robbed, many flatboats were sunk by the pirates. Their wrecks could be seen along the riverbank.

SEAFARING AND STORMS

Sailors needed great skill and seamanship to survive mountainous waves and fierce hurricanes on the high seas. This was especially true for pirates who, as outlaws, could rarely find a safe harbor to shelter in and wait for the storm to pass. Taking down the sails, facing into the storm, or sheltering close to land might help, but many pirates died when their ships capsized.

A vessel called the *Whydah Gally*—the flagship of English pirate Captain Samuel "Black Sam" Bellamy—was sunk in April 1717 off the coast of Massachusetts in a violent storm. Just two months after she'd been captured, waves measuring 40 feet high threw the ship onto a sandbar and 144 pirates and prisoners sank to a watery grave, with one of the largest hauls of gold, silver, and precious merchandise ever seized by a pirate.

10 THINGS TO SPOT

18 GUNS The *Whydah* was a 300-ton ship with 18 cannons—nine on either side.

DOWN SAILS! The risk of capsizing could be reduced by taking the sails down and running with "bare poles."

BATTEN DOWN THE HATCHES The crew tried to make the ship watertight to keep the sea from getting into the hold of the ship.

DASHING FIGURE Captain Bellamy was a dashing figure—tall, with long, dark hair and known for dressing in expensive coats.

SPANISH DOUBLOONS *The Whydah* had been captured from the Spanish only two months earlier and her hold was full of Spanish gold coins in wooden chests.

POUNDS STERLING 180 sacks of British silver coins were also on board.

ROYAL COLOR She was carrying barrels of precious indigo dye, which was one of the most expensive clothing colors at the time, worn mainly by royalty and the Church.

SHIP'S BELL With a storm brewing, the watch would have been changed every 30 minutes. Ringing the ship's bell called the next man on deck for watch duty.

LASHED TO THE HELM The helm was the wheel used to steer the ship. In bad weather, the navigator tied himself to it in case a wave washed him overboard.

SEA ANCHOR The crew would have been dragging a sea anchor behind to help stabilize the ship and keep it heading into the wind.

10 THINGS TO SPOT

 WATERY HOME Old wrecks make a perfect habitat for many sea creatures like sharks and giant moray eels.

 GOOD REEF Attaching itself to the pieces of the wrecked ship, coral can slowly cover it, creating a colorful underwater reef.

 MINI SUB The treasure may be worth millions of dollars, so divers use high-tech equipment to find it. This can include deep-sea miniature submarines.

 ECHOLOCATION Sonar, a kind of underwater radar, is used to help locate precious objects hidden beneath the water or buried in sand.

TREASURE HUNTERS

Over the centuries, hundreds of pirate ships were sunk. They may have been lost in ferocious storms, like the *Whydah Gally*, run aground, or been damaged while fighting other ships. Many carried a fortune in treasure, which now lies on the seabed waiting to be discovered. After being underwater for so long, most of a ship will probably have rotted away, but gold and silver items can survive underwater and may be undamaged.

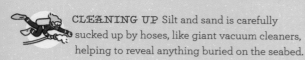

CLEANING UP Silt and sand is carefully sucked up by hoses, like giant vacuum cleaners, helping to reveal anything buried on the seabed.

OLD BONES Some of the discoveries can be a bit gruesome. Most pirates couldn't swim and drowned when their ships went down.

PRECIOUS METALS Precious metals, such as gold and silver, don't rust. Once cleaned, they can still look brand-new after hundreds of years.

BUT WHY? Marine archaeologists work with the divers to identify discoveries, record where they're found, and figure out why the ship sank.

A PIRATE'S LIFE Ordinary objects, such as cutlery, grappling hooks, or belt buckles help us to understand what life was like for pirates.

REEL 'EM IN Large, heavy objects, such as cannons or the ship's bell, are winched to the surface and onto the divers' support vessel.

Sometimes lucky divers or underwater explorers locate a ship by chance, but usually it takes years of patience and hard work to find the right clues. It took more than 250 years to find the wreckage of the *Whydah*. Using old charts or ships' logs, modern treasure hunters try to figure out precisely where each ship was before disaster struck, but over the centuries, the ocean tides and strong currents scatter the remains and cover them in sand, so they stay hidden.

A ROGUES GALLERY

We've only been able to talk about a handful of the pirates who scoured the high seas in search of wealth and infamy during the Golden Age of Piracy so far in this book. Unfortunately for the merchants, seaman, and passengers traveling the waves at the time, there were many more pirating rogues and dangerous individuals on the prowl in that era of sail ships and ocean travel. Here is a selection of a few more of them . . .

THOMAS ANSTIS
Died in 1723
This English pirate was mostly active in the Caribbean. He first took command after leading a mutiny and stealing his captain's ship.

ADAM BALDRIDGE
Disappeared in 1697
Baldridge established a pirate settlement called Ile Saint-Marie on the island of Madagascar that was a safe haven for pirates.

GEORGE BOOTH
Died in 1700
One of the first pirates to attack ships in the Indian Ocean and Red Sea rather than the Caribbean.

SAMUEL BELLAMY
1689-1717
Known as "Black Sam," in just over a year Bellamy captured more than 50 ships and stole 5 tons of treasure.

LANCELOT BLACKBURNE
1658-1743
An English priest who became Archbishop of York, Blackburne is rumored to have been a pirate, too.

STEDE BONNET
1688-1718
A rich landowner who turned to piracy, Bonnet sailed around Barbados but was eventually caught and hanged in America.

CHING SHIH
1775-1844
Known as the Pirate Queen, Madame Ching is thought to have commanded hundreds of ships and thousands of crewmen.

NICHOLAS BROWN
Died in 1726
Captured off Jamaica by a childhood friend, Brown's head was cut off and pickled so his captor could claim a large reward.

CHRISTOPHER CONDENT
Died in 1770
A successful pirate in the Indian Ocean who retired to France as a respected merchant.

JOHN EVANS
Died around 1723

Evans was an ordinary sailor in Jamaica who turned to piracy. His crew used small canoes to raid isolated coastal villages.

INGELA GATHENHIELM
1692-1729

When her privateer husband died, Ingela took over his ship and looted vessels in the Baltic Sea.

FRANÇOIS L'OLONNAIS
Died around 1668

A French servant turned pirate who once escaped his enemies by pretending to be dead.

JOHN RACKHAM
1682-1720

A pirate in the West Indies, he was known as "Calico Jack" because of his colorful cotton clothing.

JOHN JULIAN
Died in 1733

Part Native American and descended from an African slave, Julian was the first black pirate to be recorded on the American coast.

MARIA LINDSEY
1700-1760

Lindsey was born in England, but she and her husband worked as pirates in Canada before fleeing to France.

JOHN KING
1706-1717

Active in the Caribbean, King was the youngest known pirate. He may have been as young as eight when he first went to sea.

HAYREDDIN BARBAROSSA
1478-1546

Barbarossa ("Redbeard") and his older brother, Oruc, were corsairs fighting for the Ottoman sultan.

CHARLES VANE
1680-1720

Sailing around the Bahamas, Vane was cruel to his crew and prisoners. Ignoring the Pirate Code, he refused to share his treasure.

RACHEL WALL
1760-1789

Raiding along the coast of New Hampshire, Wall is thought to have been America's first female pirate.

SIR FRANCIS DRAKE
1540-96

A hero in England, Drake was no more than a pirate to the Spanish, whose king offered a huge reward for his capture, dead or alive.

RAIS HAMIDOU
1773-1815

This Algerian pirate captured many ships and European slaves during his career. He was killed in a battle against the American navy.

CAN YOU FIND?

Take a look at the items below and see if you can remember in which scene you saw them. Or, if you haven't seen them before, now is your chance to hunt them down by returning to each action-packed scene for a second look. Don't forget to use your magnifying glass so that you can study the finer detail in each spread. You'll be surprised what else you missed the first time around.

A Komodo dragon

Flying fish

*Victim tied
to the deck*

Gold-loving octopus

*Pirate on
the mast*

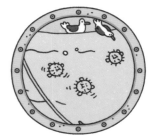

"High-fiving" octopus

Dancing pig

*Handing down
the loot*

*Weighing
the gold*

Spiky puffer fish

Skinny-dipping pirates

*Captive in
a rug!*

Pirate asleep under a tree

Walking the anchor chain

Eeeeek!

"It's my rug!"

A hiding fox

Stealing the cannonballs

*Wrestling
a crocodile*

*Fire on
board!*

Sunbathing seal

*Running away with
the candlesticks*

Goat on a rooftop

*Smoking a pipe
on deck*

Climbing the mast

*Playing guitar on
the shore*

The ship's cat

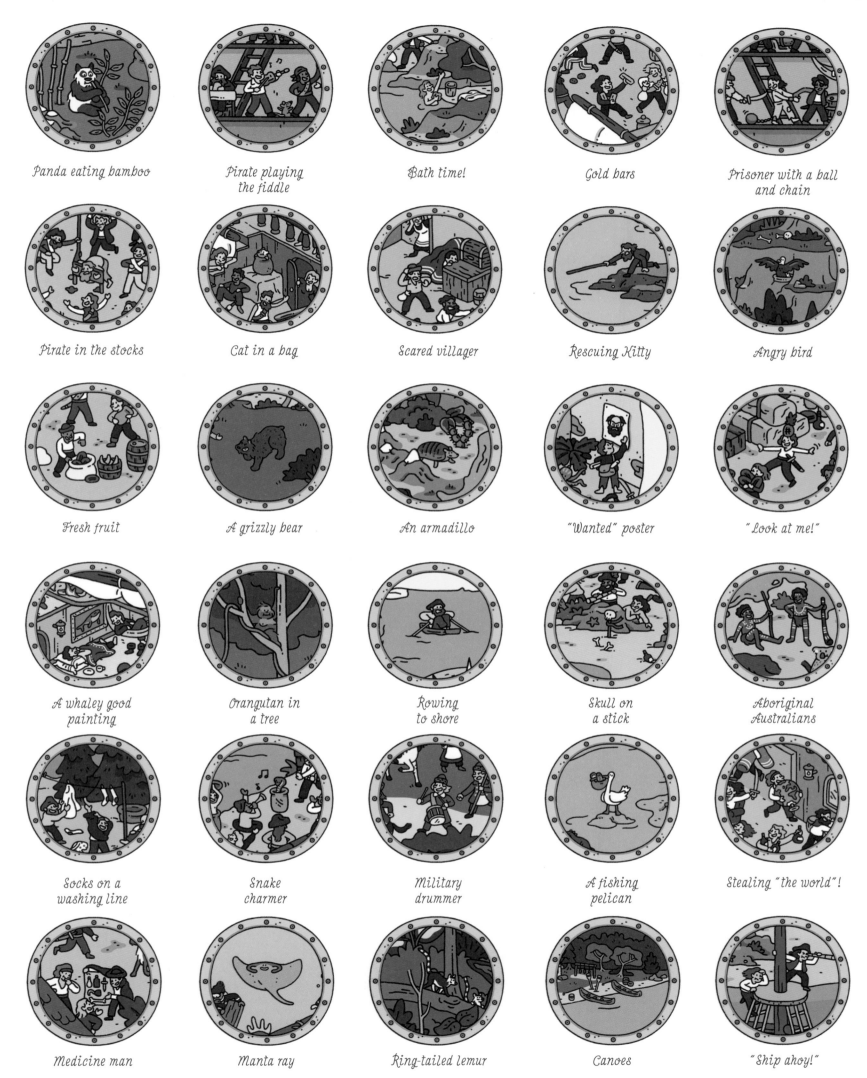

Panda eating bamboo

Pirate playing
the fiddle

Bath time!

Gold bars

Prisoner with a ball
and chain

Pirate in the stocks

Cat in a bag

Scared villager

Rescuing Kitty

Angry bird

Fresh fruit

A grizzly bear

An armadillo

"Wanted" poster

"Look at me!"

A whaley good
painting

Orangutan in
a tree

Rowing
to shore

Skull on
a stick

Aboriginal
Australians

Socks on a
washing line

Snake
charmer

Military
drummer

A fishing
pelican

Stealing "the world"!

Medicine man

Manta ray

Ring-tailed lemur

Canoes

"Ship ahoy!"

ANSWERS

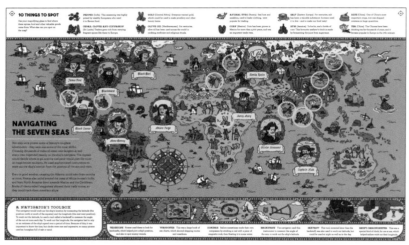

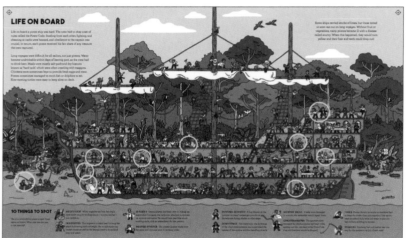

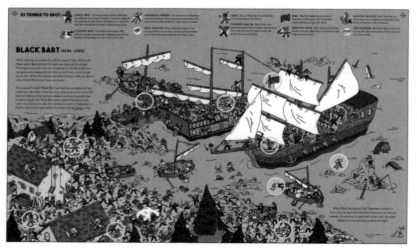

BLACK CAESAR (1690-1718)

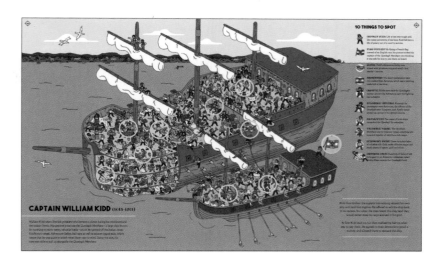

CAPTAIN WILLIAM KIDD (1645-1701)

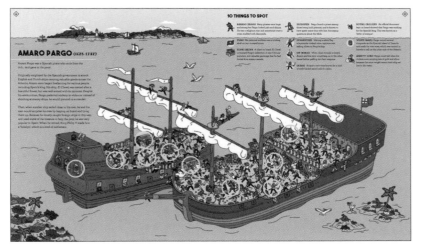

AMARO PARGO (1678-1747)

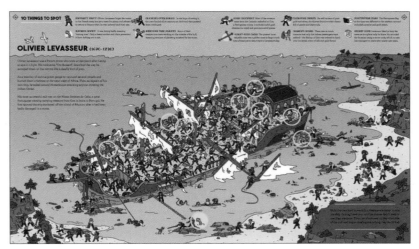

OLIVIER LEVASSEUR (1690-1730)

STENKA RAZIN (1630-1671)

JAMES FORD (1775-1833)

SEAFARING AND STORMS

TREASURE HUNTERS

TALK LIKE A PIRATE

Anyone can talk like a pirate, but just in case you landlubbers need a bit o' tellin', here's a quick lesson in the language of skulduggery . . .

GENERAL RULES

1. SIMPLE SWAPS:
- My becomes "me"
- You becomes "ye"
- Yours becomes "yer"

2. DROP LETTERS:
- Going becomes goin'; doing becomes doin', etc.
- Right becomes "ri" (said "rye")
- Forgotten becomes "forgot"
- And becomes "n"

3. BE LOUD AND DON'T FORGET TO SWAGGER.

4. USE SEAFARING REFERENCES:
- Old would be "barnacle-covered" or "crusty"
- Smells like a wet dog would become "smells like a dank sea monster!"

5. BE IMAGINATIVE WITH INSULTS. Involve animals, illnesses, or bad odors: "Ye mangy ol' sewer rat," or "May the pox be upon ye!"

6. MUTTER AND MUMBLE LOTS.

WHY NOT GIVE IT A TRY . . .

I've forgotten my lunch money =
FORGOT THEM DOUBLOONS FOR ME VITTLES!

What time is it? =
WHAT HOUR BE IT?

He was very old =
'E WAS EX'RA BARNACLE-COVERED

A–Z OF PIRATE SLANG

AHOY
Hello

AHOY, MATEY
Hello, friend

AHOY, ME HEARTIES
Hello, my friends

ALL HANDS HOAY
Everyone get on the deck

AAARRRGGGHHH!
Said every other word

AVAST YE
Stop and check this out / pay attention

AYE
Yes

BATTEN DOWN THE HATCHES
Prepare the ship, a storm is brewing

BARNACLE-COVERED
Old

BILGE-SUCKING
An insult

BLACK SPOT
A curse

BLIMEY!
Exclamation of surprise

BLOW ME DOWN!
Expression of shock or disbelief

CACKLE FRUIT
Chicken eggs

DANCE THE HEMPEN JIG
To hang

DAVY JONES'S LOCKER
Dead

DEAD MEN TELL NO TALES
Leave no one alive!

FEED THE FISH
A prediction that someone is about to die

HANG 'IM FROM THE YARDARM
A punishment for prisoners

HEAVE HO
Put some effort into something

HEMPEN HALTER
The noose used for hanging

HORNSWOGGLE
To cheat or be cheated

JUMP SHIP
Abandon ship without the captain's permission

LANDLUBBER
A person who doesn't know how to sail

MAY THE POX BE UPON YE!
A curse (wishing smallpox upon someone . . . Nasty!)

OLD SALT
A sailor with a lot of experience at sea

SCALLYWAG
An insult

SCUTTLE
To sink a ship

SEADOG
An old sailor or pirate

SEWER RAT
An insult

SHARK BAIT
Going to die soon

SHIVER ME TIMBERS
An expression used to show shock or disbelief

SHIPSHAPE
Clean and orderly

SKULDUGGERY
Normal dishonest, unscrupulous pirate behavior

SON OF A BISCUIT EATER
An insult

SCURVY DOG
An insult

SPLICE THE MAINBRACE!
Give the crew a drink (of rum, naturally!)

THAR SHE BLOWS!
I've spotted a whale

THREE SHEETS TO THE WIND
Someone who is drunk

VITTLES
Food

WALK THE PLANK
A punishment whereby someone walks a plank until they fall into the sea, which usually ends with a visit to Davy Jones's Locker

WEIGH ANCHOR AND HOIST THE MIZZEN!
Let's go (pull up the anchor and set the sail)!

YO-HO-HO!
Cheerful outburst

GLOSSARY

BLUNDERBUSS
a short gun with a wide, trumpet-shaped barrel

BOOTY
treasure

BROADSIDE
firing all the cannons on one side of a ship

BUCCANEERS
people who join forces with other pirates to carry out bigger raids

CHRONOMETER
a special kind of ship's clock

CORSAIR
a pirate in the Mediterranean Sea

CUTLASS
a short, heavy type of saber

DOUBLOON
a Spanish gold coin

FARMSTEAD
a farm and all its outbuildings

FLINTLOCK PISTOL
a type of gun with a flint that sparks the gunpowder

GALLOWS
a wooden structure for hanging criminals

GRAPPLING IRONS
ropes and hooks used to climb aboard a ship

LETTER OF MARQUE
an official letter from a government or monarch, giving a privateer permission to attack foreign ships

MERCHANT
a person involved in buying and selling

MUSKET
a long-barrelled gun, fired from the shoulder

NAVIGATOR
the person who plots a course and steers the ship

PIECE OF EIGHT
a Spanish silver coin

PLUNDER OR LOOT
to rob and steal (also the spoils from robbing and stealing)

PORT ROYAL, JAMAICA
the center of trade in the Caribbean during the "Golden Age of Piracy," and a hotspot for pirates

POWDER MONKEY
a young boy who carries gunpowder during an attack

PRIVATEER
government-sponsored pirate

SABER
a long, curved sword usually with a round metal knuckle guard

SCURVY
a disease caused by a lack of vitamin C, which is found in fruit and vegetables. Most pirates had it!

SEXTANT
a navigational instrument, which calculates the position of the sun above the horizon

SHASHKA
a Russian sword similar to a saber, but without a hand guard

SKULL AND CROSSBONES OR JOLLY ROGER
the traditional pirate flag

SWABBIES
pirates who mop the decks

SWIVEL GUN
a small cannon mounted on a swiveling stand

THE BOATSWAIN
the person who inspects the ship every morning to make sure it is "shipshape"

THE CAPTAIN
the person in charge on board a ship

THE PIRATE CODE
the rules of being a pirate (division of booty, discipline, jobs on deck)

THE QUARTERMASTER
the person who keeps order on board ship and "flogs" any pirate who breaks the Pirate Code

WAGGONER
a large book of sea charts used by pirates for navigation

SHIP TERMS

BOW
the front of a ship

BRIG
a two-masted, square-rigged ship

CROW'S NEST
small lookout platform atop the mast

HULL
the main body of the ship (sloops have shallow hulls so they can sail close to shore without running aground)

JIB
a triangular sail set in front of the main sail

MAINSAIL
erm … the "main sail" of a ship

MID-SHIP
the middle of the ship

POOP DECK
the deck that is highest and farthest back on a ship

PORT
the left side of a ship (facing forward)

RIGGING
the system of ropes or chains supporting the ship's masts and used to control the sails

SLOOP
a one-masted, square-rigged ship favored by pirates because it is small and fast

STARBOARD
the right side of the ship

STERN
the back of a ship

YARDARM
the horizontal beam on a square-rigged ship